Amazing Animals
Pigs

Please visit our web site at www.garethstevens.com
For a free catalog describing our list of high-quality books, call 1-800-542-2595 (USA) or 1-800-387-3178 (Canada).
Our fax: 1-877-542-2596

Library of Congress Cataloging-in-Publication Data

Wilsdon, Christina.
    Pigs / by Christina Wilsdon.
          p. cm. — (Amazing animals)
    Originally published: Pleasantville, NY: Reader's Digest Young Families, c2007.
    Includes bibliographical references and index.
    ISBN-10: 0-8368-9122-8   ISBN-13: 978-0-8368-9122-5 (lib. bdg.)
    ISBN-10: 1-4339-2126-X   ISBN-13: 978-1-4339-2126-1 (soft cover)
    1. Swine—Juvenile literature. I. Title.
    SF395.5.W55 2009
    636.4—dc22   2009003929

This edition first published in 2010 by
Gareth Stevens Publishing
A Weekly Reader® Company
1 Reader's Digest Road
Pleasantville, NY 10570-7000 USA

Executive Managing Editor: Lisa M. Herrington
Senior Editor: Brian Fitzgerald
Senior Designer: Keith Plechaty

Produced by Editorial Directions, Inc.
Art Direction and Page Production: The Design Lab/Kathleen Petelinsek and Gregory Lindholm
Consultant: Robert E. Budliger (Retired), NY State Department of Environmental Conservation

Photo Credits
Cover: Image Source; title page: iStockphoto.com/Rob Sylvan; contents page: Image Source; pages 6–7: Corbis; page 8: iStockphoto.com/Jeffery Hockstrasser; page 10: iStockphoto.com/Mark Stokes; page 11: iStockphoto.com/Tammy Michaels; page 12: Shawn Hine/Shutterstock Inc.; page 13: iStockphoto.com/Craig Walsh; pages 14–15: Corbis; page 16: Nova Development Corporation; page 19: Tiberius Dinu/Shutterstock Inc.; page 20: Ariusz Nawrocki/Shutterstock Inc.; pages 22–23: Louis Caldwell/Shutterstock Inc.; page 24: Nicholas Rjabow/Shutterstock Inc.; page 26: Steve Mann/Shutterstock Inc.; page 27: iStockphoto.com/Christopher Messer; page 28: John Peters/Shutterstock Inc.; pages 30–31: Doxa/Shutterstock Inc.; page 32: Ivan Thielka/Shutterstock Inc.; page 33: Greg Toope/Shutterstock Inc.; page 34: Ecoprint/Shutterstock Inc.; page 35: Doxa/Shutterstock Inc.; page 36: Anita Huszti/Shutterstock Inc.; pages 38–39: Corbis; page 40: Corbis; page 43: Wendy M. Simmons/Shutterstock Inc.; pages 44–45: Image Source; page 46: Steve Mann/Shutterstock Inc.; back cover: iStockphoto.com/Rob Sylvan.

Printed in the United States of America

1 2 3 4 5 6 7 8 9 14 13 12 11 10 09

Amazing Animals
Pigs

By Christina Wilsdon

Gareth Stevens
Publishing

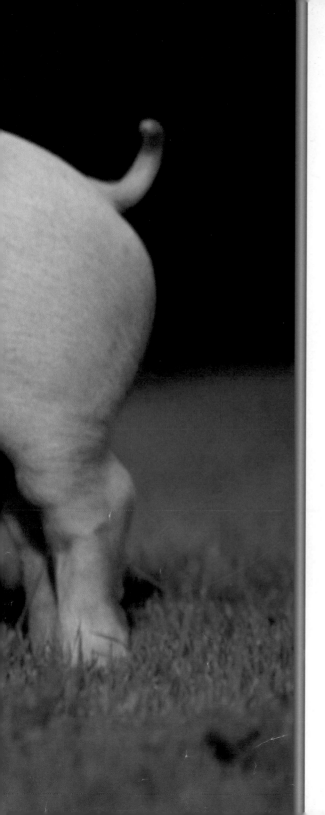

Contents

Chapter 1
A Pig Story

Bundles of Joy

A mother pig can have as many as 12 babies at one time. Some kinds of pigs have 15 or more. A few pigs have given birth to more than 30 **piglets** in one **litter**! The piglets born first start drinking milk from the mother pig even before their younger brothers and sisters are born.

The mother pig grunted softly as she pushed straw into a pile with her nose, or **snout**. Then she flopped onto the pile with a sigh. The mother had made a cozy nest in the hut. Now she was ready to give birth.

The baby pigs arrived quickly—all 12 of them! They crowded against their mother's belly. Along her belly were two rows of teats, which held milk. The teats near the mother's front legs offered the most milk. The baby pigs fought to get those spots. They shoved and jostled each other. They pushed with their snouts and toes, which are called hooves.

Soon the strongest baby pigs won the best places. They began to drink. Farther down the mother's belly, the other baby pigs also settled in to drink. The mother pig grunted as they nursed.

After all that work, it was time for a nap. The piglets snuggled up in the straw. A heat lamp provided extra warmth for them.

Wild Words

A male pig is called a **boar**. A female pig that has had babies is called a **sow**. A baby pig is called a piglet. A family of piglets is called a litter.

The biggest piglet claimed the spot right behind his mother's left front leg. He was the first pig to take a peek outside the hut.

Other pigs lived in little huts, too. The huts were scattered across a big field. The pigs were free to go in and out of them. For now, though, the baby pigs stayed in a little fenced yard next to their hut.

The little yard was filled with straw. The big piglet loved to dig in the straw and push it around with his snout.

The piglet also played with his brothers and sisters. They scampered and leaped about. They nipped at each other and pushed each other over.

The farmer gave the baby pigs special toys. She hung bits of old rubber hose and strips of cloth above the pen. The big piglet loved to chew on the hoses and tug on the cloth. Sometimes the farmer gave them a ball to roll!

When playtime was over, the piglet and most of his brothers and sisters flopped down into a pink pile to nap. The others stayed with the mother pig.

At first the piglets' only food was their mother's milk. Then when the piglets were about a week old, the farmer began feeding them special "pig chow." The chow looked like the dry **kibble** cats and dogs eat. The farmer poured it into a long, narrow tray, called a trough (TRAWF).

The big piglet grew fast. He weighed about 3 pounds (1 kilogram) when he was born. Then, at the age of five weeks, he weighed about 15 pounds (7 kg). The baby pigs were old enough to go outside with their mother. They **rooted** in the dirt for good things to eat. They ran and played, squealing and oinking. On hot days, they lay in cool dirt or mud. They huddled in straw inside their hut when it was chilly.

By the time he is six months old, the piglet will be half the size of his mother. He will weigh about 220 pounds (100 kg)—as much as a newborn baby elephant!

This Little Piggy ...

Sometimes a litter of piglets includes tiny babies that are only half the size of the others. A piglet that is very small is called a runt. A runt may be too weak and small to get its fair share of milk. Runts are often removed from the litter and raised separately.

Chapter 2
The Body of a Pig

A sow lets her piglets nurse for 6 to 10 weeks after their birth. After that, she will push them away.

Pick a Pig

There are about 500 **breeds** of **domestic** pigs. Some kinds have long, lean bodies. Others are plump and round. All pigs look a bit like barrels with legs. Each leg has four hooves, but the pig walks only on the middle two hooves.

The Whole Hog

A pig's skin is thick but sensitive. A white-skinned pig can get sunburned. A pig can also get too hot very quickly. It cannot sweat to cool off. It must soak itself in a puddle or mud hole instead.

Bristly hair grows on a pig's skin. Pigs that live in the wild have longer, thicker hair than farm pigs. Some pigs have very little hair.

How Now, Brown Sow!

Many pigs are pink. But pigs are also black, white, brown, red, red-yellow, and blue-gray, or they can be a mixture of colors.

Some kinds of pigs always have certain patterns. Spotted Poland pigs are white with black spots. Berkshire pigs are black with white legs, tails, and snouts. Hampshire pigs are black with a white band around their shoulders and front legs. Pigs like this are called belted pigs.

Pigs' Eyes and Ears

A pig has small eyes, and it can't see very well. It hears just fine, though. Some kinds of pigs have short, perky ears that stick up. Others have long ears that droop. Some have extra-long, extra-droopy ears called lop ears.

About Snouts

A pig's snout is strong and flexible. A pig uses its snout like a plow, to dig in the dirt and find food. At the end of the snout is a rubbery pad with a pair of nostrils. This pad is very sensitive to touch. A pig uses its snout to feel for things to eat as it **snuffles** along the ground. Its sense of smell is also very sharp. A pig can smell buried food that is 20 feet (6 meters) away.

Noisy Oinkers

Pigs can be noisy. They oink, grunt, and snort. They squeal when they are excited or scared. Scientists have measured a pig's squeal. They found that it was louder than music at a rock concert!

The noises pigs make have earned them the nicknames "oinkers" and "grunters."

Pigs sometimes wag their tails as they nurse from their mother or eat from a trough.

A Pig's Tail

Pigs that live in the wild have straight tails. Farm pigs have curly tails, but they can uncurl them. A relaxed pig may let its tail hang down. An alert pig curls its tail and holds it up on its back.

Baby pigs often bite one another's tails when they play or fight. Sometimes farmers shorten piglets' tails to keep the piglets from hurting one another.

Big Pigs, Little Pigs

All piglets grow quickly, but different kinds of pigs grow to be different sizes. Some fully grown farm pigs weigh 400 to 500 pounds (181 to 227 kg). Other pigs grow even larger and weigh more than 600 pounds (272 kg).

Some Big Pig!

The biggest pig on record was a Poland China hog named Big Bill. He weighed 2,552 pounds (1,158 kg)—about as much as a passenger car. He measured 9 feet long (274 centimeters) from snout to tail—as long as three yardsticks laid end to end. When fully grown, most Poland China pigs weigh less than half as much as Big Bill.

Chapter 3
What Pigs Do

A pig snuffles its snout and roots around in the dirt or any kind of ground cover to look for food.

Pigging Out

Have you ever heard the phrase "eating like a pig"? A person who eats like a pig is eating too much or eating sloppily—or both!

Pigs do eat sloppily. The food that is fed to a pig on a small farm is even called **slops**! However, pigs do not overeat. They eat only what they need. A pig growing up on a pig farm eats from 5 to 8 pounds (2 to 4 kg) of food a day. Its meals include grains such as corn and wheat. Pigs may also eat a special pig chow made from grains and mixed with vitamins, minerals, and proteins. A pig raised by a family may get leftovers from the table as well.

A pig that is allowed to root in the dirt outdoors finds other tasty tidbits. It eats the same things that pigs in the wild eat—roots, seeds, leaves, fruits, nuts, mushrooms, worms, insects, slugs, snails, and mice.

Come and Get It!

Have you ever called a dog or cat to come and get its dinner? People who keep pigs on small farms may call their pigs to meals, too. A common way of calling them is to shout "Sooie!" Some people also call "Here, pig, pig, pig!" Hog-calling contests are a popular feature at many county fairs.

Pigs at Rest

A farm pig spends about two hours a day eating. A wild pig spends about seven hours a day eating because it works harder to find food.

What does a pig do with the rest of its time? Mostly, it sleeps! A pig sleeps from 11 to 13 hours a day. A sleepy pig flops down on its side to snooze. Even its curly tail relaxes.

Pigs at Play

Pigs are clever animals. They can learn tricks easily. Scientists have found that pigs are as smart as cats and dogs, if not smarter!

Pigs that can go outdoors find plenty to do. They spend lots of time rooting in the dirt. But pigs that are raised indoors in pens can get bored. They may bite one another if they do not have something better to do.

So farmers give indoor pigs lots of hay. The pigs spend lots of time rooting in it. Farmers also give pigs toys. They hang strips of cloth and sections of rubber hose over the pen for pigs to chew and tug on.

Pigs will flop down and stretch out to take a nap anytime, anywhere.

Lying in mud keeps a pig cool and protects its skin from sunburn and biting insects.

Mud Baths

Pigs are famous for being dirty, but they are actually clean animals. A pig in a pen keeps its home cleaner than a horse or cow does. It sleeps in one area and goes to the bathroom in a different area. It will not play with a ball or other toy that is very dirty.

What about all the pictures of pigs in mud puddles? A pig taking a mud bath is not trying to get dirty. It is trying to keep cool. A pig does not have sweat glands, so it cannot sweat to cool off. It must use water outside its body to cool down.

A pig will choose a clean, damp patch of dirt or a puddle of water if it can. It will loll in mud only if that is all there is. Spending time in a puddle or a mud hole is called **wallowing**.

Farmers cool off pigs that live indoors with fine-mist sprinklers and fans. Farmers also spray them with a garden hose.

Blue Ribbon Winners!

Some people enter their pigs in pig shows at fairs. The pigs are judged on their overall appearance. The owners scrub the pigs until they are squeaky clean. They even shave the hair from the pigs' ears and tails to make them look extra-tidy!

Chapter 4

Pigs in the Wild

The wild boar is the "great-granddaddy," or ancient relative, of most kinds of farm pigs.

What a Boar!

Most pigs are farm pigs. However, there are some pigs that still root and grunt in the wild. One of these wild pigs is the wild boar.

A wild boar has long legs and strong shoulders. Thick, bristly hair covers its body. Two of its upper teeth, called **tusks**, grow out of its mouth. Tusks may be 3 to 5 inches (8 to 13 cm) long. Two lower teeth stick out of a boar's mouth, too.

Wild boars once lived only in Europe, Asia, and part of Africa. Then people brought wild boars to almost every land they visited. They set them free so they could be hunted for food. Wild boars now live in parts of North and South America and in Australia, too. They can survive in woods and fields as well as rain forests and dry places. Their favorite foods are nuts and acorns. They also eat fruit, insects, worms, lizards, eggs, mice, and baby deer.

Baby Boarlets

Baby wild boars are called boarlets. Their fur is striped brown and tan. The stripes protect the boarlets by helping them blend in with plants. Boarlets lose their stripes when they are about three months old.

Bumps on a Hog

The warthog is a cousin of wild boars and farm pigs. Its **habitat** is the grasslands of Africa. This pig gets its name from its face, which has four big bumps. These bumps are very big on a male warthog's face. They help protect him when he fights with other male warthogs.

A warthog can run up to 35 miles (56 kilometers) per hour. It needs this speed to run away from lions, leopards, and cheetahs, which are the warthog's main **predators**. The warthog holds its tail straight up in the air when it runs.

Warthogs eat mainly grass. They kneel down on their front legs to graze. They do not usually root for food as farm pigs do. They can also handle hotter weather than farm pigs can. But warthogs will gladly wallow in mud whenever they get the chance!

Warthogs sleep in underground dens. Usually the den is an old burrow that was made by another animal. If a warthog can't find an old den, it may dig out a hollow under a bush. A warthog will also hide from danger in its den. It always goes into its den tail first. That way, any animal that dares to enter its den will meet a face full of sharp tusks!

Both male and female warthogs have tusks. An old male's tusks may grow to be as long as 12 inches (30 cm).

Some feral pigs look a lot like wild boars. Others look like a cross between a boar and a farm pig.

Hog Wild

Many pigs that run free in woods, forests, and fields are not really members of a wild **species** of pig. They are relatives of pigs that escaped from farms long ago, and they are called **feral** pigs. Runaway pigs survive very well in the wild because they eat so many kinds of foods.

Feral pigs are a problem in many places. Pigs root to find food. Their wallowing makes puddles and mud holes larger. Rooting and wallowing destroy the plants that grow in these spots. Then there are no roots to hold the soil in place. When rain falls, the soil washes away.

Feral pigs also eat the roots of plants, killing them. This makes it easier for weeds to grow. The weeds take over the soil and leave no room for other kinds of plants. Without the plants, other wild animals in the area do not have the food and shelter they need.

In Hawaii, feral pigs have damaged many wild areas. They have turned parts of rain forests into weedy, muddy patches. Mosquitoes come to lay eggs in these wet patches, spreading a disease that has killed many Hawaiian birds. Building fences and hunting are two ways people control feral pigs.

Chapter 5
Pigs and People

There are about
one billion farm pigs
in the world today.

Hog History

The world's first wild pigs lived about 40 million years ago—long after the last dinosaurs died out.

About 9,000 years ago, people started to tame pigs and raise them for food. Over time, the farm pigs became different from wild pigs in many ways. They looked different and were tamer. An animal that goes through changes like this is called a domesticated animal. Pigs were probably first domesticated in the Middle East and then in China.

Pigs as Pork

Almost half of the world's farm pigs are raised in China. Farmers in the United States raise about 60 million pigs a year. Farm pigs are used as food. Meat from pigs is called pork, and pig farmers are called pork producers. Pork chops, bacon, ham, bologna, and pork sausages all come from pigs.

Other parts of pigs are used to make other products. Pigskin is made into shoes, gloves, and other clothing. Hog hair is used to make bristles for brushes. Some medical supplies are made from pig parts. Even the pig's fat, blood, and bones are used. Farmers often say that when it comes to pigs, you can use "everything but the oink"!

Pigs as Pets

Today, some people keep pigs as pets. The most popular pet pig is the Vietnamese potbelly. Potbellies are named for their round tummies that nearly drag on the ground. They have short legs, short noses, and wrinkly skin. A potbelly pig can grow to be 150 to 200 pounds (68 to 91 kg). A potbelly can be trained to use a litter box like a cat. It can learn tricks, too.

Pigs at Work!

The pig's appetite has allowed people to use pigs as a cleanup crew. In ancient times, people let pigs wander freely in villages to feed on garbage. In the past, farmers also let pigs root in fields. The pigs ate weeds and dug up the soil, which helped get it ready for planting a new crop. In France and Italy, pigs are sometimes used to find truffles—rare, tasty fungi that grow about 12 inches (30 cm) underground.

A Rare Pig

Some of the pig's wild cousins are rare. The rarest is the pygmy hog, which lives in a part of India. This tiny pig weighs only 14 to 22 pounds (6 to 10 kg). The pygmy hog is rare because there is not much left of the vast grasslands where it once roamed.

A pig can be a great family pet. It can be trained easily. It readily gives and accepts affection.

Glossary

boar—an adult male pig

breeds—different varieties of the same animal species

domestic—describing animals that have been bred over time to be tame companions and farm animals

feral—domestic animals that are no longer tame and live in the wild

habitat—the natural environment where an animal or a plant lives

kibble—small bits of food made especially for an animal to eat

litter—a family of piglets

Fast Facts About the Farm Pig

Scientific name	*Sus scrofa domesticus*
Class	Mammals
Order	Artiodactyla
Size	Males: up to 6 feet (183 cm) in length, depending on breed
Weight	150–1,500 pounds (68–680 kg), depending on breed and age
Height	1–4 feet (30–122 cm), depending on breed
Life span	Up to 21 years
Habitat	Farm

piglet—a baby pig

predator—an animal that hunts and eats other animals to survive

root—to push around and dig in dirt using the snout

slops—meals for pigs

snout—the part of an animal's head where the nose and jaws stick out in front

snuffle—to breathe in to smell something

sow—an adult female pig

species—a group of living things that are the same in many ways

tusk—a long, pointed tooth that sticks far out from an animal's mouth

wallow—to lie in water or mud to cool off

Pigs: Show What You Know

How much have you learned about pigs? Grab a piece of paper and a pencil and write your answers down.

1. What is another name for a family of piglets?

2. How much do baby farm pigs weigh when they are first born?

3. What does it mean when a pig curls its tail and holds it up on its back?

4. How many breeds of domestic pigs are there?

5. How much time does a pig spend sleeping each day?

6. Why do pigs spend time in puddles of water or mud?

7. How fast can a warthog run?

8. What are feral pigs?

9. When did people start taming pigs and raising them for food?

10. What is the most popular type of pig for people to keep as a pet?

1. A litter 2. About 3 pounds (1 kg) 3. That the pig is alert 4. About 500 5. Around 11 to 13 hours 6. Since they lack sweat glands, it is the only way they can cool off. 7. About 35 miles (56 km) per hour 8. Relatives of pigs that long ago escaped from farms and learned to live in the wild 9. About 9,000 years ago 10. The Vietnamese potbelly

For More Information

Books

Nelson, Robin. *Pigs* (Farm Animals). Minneapolis: Lerner Publications, 2009.

Rau, Dana Meachen. *Guess Who Grunts: Pig*. Tarrytown, NY: Benchmark Books, 2009.

Somervill, Barbara. *Wild Boar*. Ann Arbor, MI: Cherry Lake Publishing, 2009.

Web Sites

Barnyard Palace

www.agr.state.nc.us/cyber/kidswrld/general/barnyard/pigs.htm

Learn the life cycle, eating habits, and other cool facts about barnyard pigs.

Kidipede: Pigs

www.historyforkids.org/learn/economy/pigs.htm

Check out videos and get the history of pigs.

Publisher's note to educators and parents: Our editors have carefully reviewed these web sites to ensure that they are suitable for children. Many web sites change frequently, however, and we cannot guarantee that a site's future contents will continue to meet our high standards of quality and educational value. Be advised that children should be closely supervised whenever they access the Internet.

Index

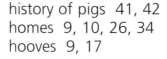